GOD'S BUBBLY, GURGLY,

OVERWHELMING, OVERFLOWING

LOVE

GOD'S BUBBLY, GURGLY, OVERWHELMING, OVERFLOWING LOVE

written by BARBARA PAPPAS

illustrated by IRENE BOUTZARELOS

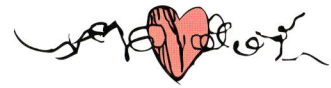

Amnos Publications
Westchester, Illinois

By the same author:

Are You Saved?
The Orthodox Christian Process of Salvation
Fourth Edition
ISBN: 0-9623721-4-5

The Christian Life in the Early Church and TODAY
According to St. Paul's First Epistle to the Corinthians
ISBN: 0-9623721-3-7

The Christian Life in the Early Church and TODAY
According to St. Paul's Second Epistle to the Corinthians
ISBN: 0-9623721-5-3

© copyright 1999 by Barbara Pappas

All rights reserved. No part of this book may be reproduced, stored in a retrieval system or transmitted in any form or by any means, electronic, mechanical, photocopying, recording or otherwise, without written permission, except by a reviewer who may quote brief passages in a review.

Library of Congress Catalog Card Number: 99-98133

ISBN: 0-9623721-6-1

First Edition - October 2000
1 2 3 4 5 6 7 8 9 - 08 07 06 05 04 03 02 01 00

Amnos Publications
2501 South Wolf Road
Westchester, Illinois 60154
(708)562-2744
Fax: (708)562-2752
e-mail: HARC@mediaone.net

Printed in Canada

to Maria, Michael, Justin and Jeremy
and
to all those with loving hearts and inquiring minds

THE BEGINNING

In the beginning . . .

There was no sun.

There was no sand.

There was no sea.

There was no moon.

There were no stars.

There was no you —

no me!

There was only God!!!

God was filled with *Bubbly, Gurgly, Overwhelming, Overflowing Love.*

His love bubbled and gurgled and foamed

until it finally overflowed!

Every time God's love overflowed,

something wonderful happened!

With His *Bubbly, Gurgly,*

Overwhelming, Overflowing Love,

God created spirits

to be with Him in Heaven.

He called the heavenly spirits

Angels and Archangels,

Cherubim and Seraphim.

They surrounded His throne

and sang praises to Him.

But *God's Bubbly, Gurgly, Overwhelming, Overflowing Love*

didn't stop there.

It continued to bubble and gurgle and foam.

It simmered and spattered and popped

                until it overflowed again!

This time He created the world.

God set the sun in the sky to light up the day.

He hung the moon and the stars to brighten the night.

He created tall mountains and low valleys

...and caves.

He scattered earth between rivers

and sand around seas.

Gen 1:14-18

He created the trees and the flowers

and the birds and the bees

and fish

and reptiles

and insects

and animals!

When God was finished,

He looked all around

and said: *It is good*.

It is very good!

But there was no one on earth

to enjoy the goodness.

...no one to sit in the sun

or to play in the sand.

...no one to smell the flowers

or to climb the trees.

...no one to run and to play

with the birds and the bees.

Gen 2:4-6

So God's Bubbly, Gurgly, Overwhelming, Overflowing Love

bubbled and gurgled and foamed once more.

It simmered and spattered and popped,

it gurgled and boiled and rocked...

until it overflowed again!

This time God created Adam and Eve.

They lived in Paradise—a beautiful garden called Eden.

Eden was filled with waterfalls and streams

...and wondrous forests

...and sweet scents

...and butterflies!

God gave Adam and Eve a very important task:

to take care of everything He had created.

One by one,

God brought every living creature to Adam

so he could give them their names.

Adam saw big strong animals

with golden fur around their faces.

He called them *lions*.

Adam saw velvety animals

with big black spots.

He called them *cheetahs*.

Adam saw animals with long, long necks

that reached into the tops of trees.

He called them *giraffes*.

Adam saw fat little black and white animals

with big black masks

and ringed, bushy tails.

He called them *racoons.*

Adam saw friendly little black and white birds

who love to hang upside down.

He called them *chickadees*.

Adam and Eve played with the animals

and ate from the trees.

They sang songs to God

with the birds and the bees.

God walked with them!

He talked with them!

Adam and Eve were very happy!

God's Bubbly, Gurgly, Overwhelming, Overflowing Love

filled their hearts with joy!

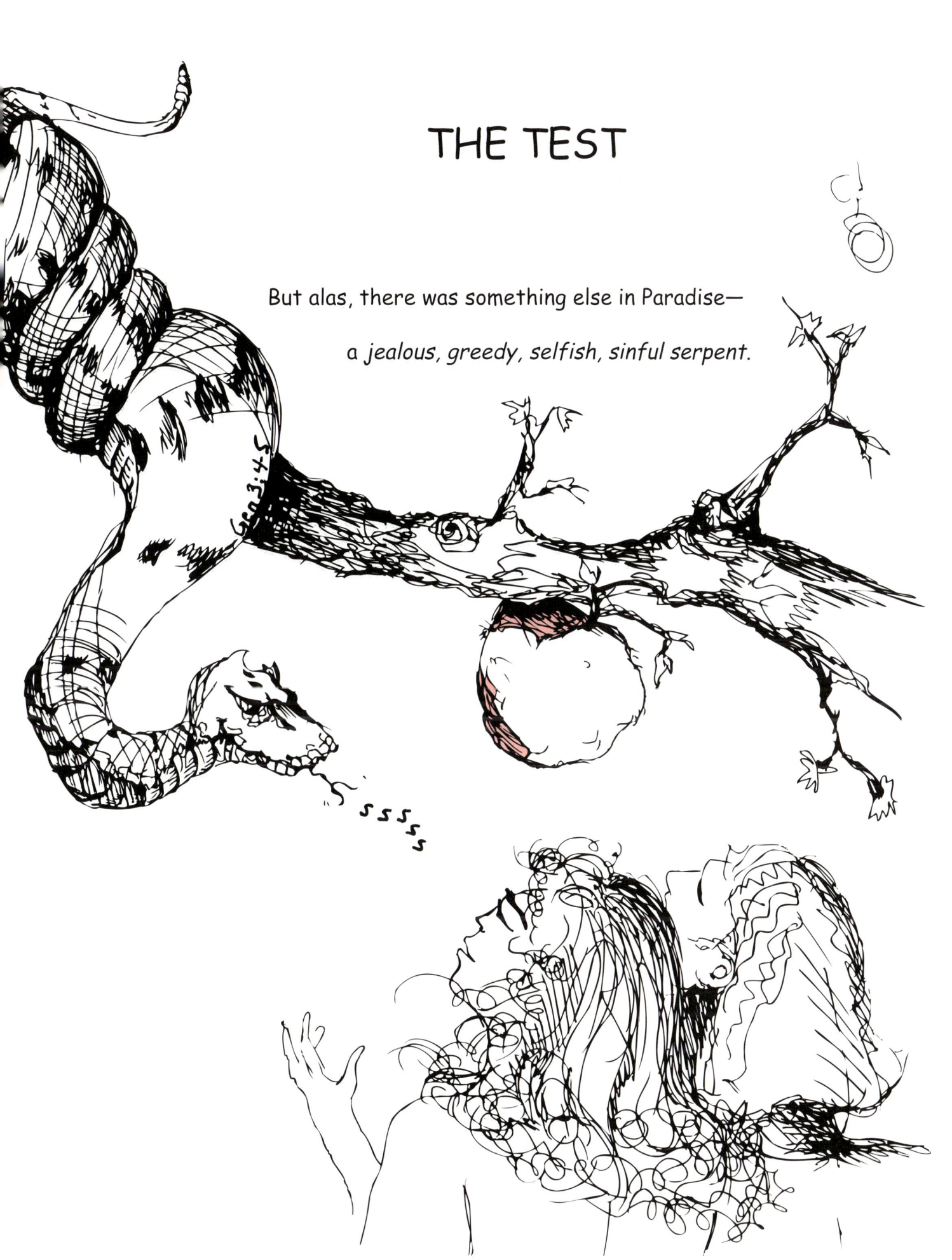

God told Adam and Eve

that they could do anything they wanted to do

in the Garden of Eden.

Well—*almost* anything!

There was one tree in Eden

  that God told them to stay away from:

    the Tree of Knowledge of Good and Evil.

God showed His love for Adam and Eve

  by giving them all of the

    wonderful things He had created.

He wanted them

  to show their love for Him

    by being obedient.

1 John 5:3

So, the next day

they went closer!

They touched the trunk of the tree!

They pulled on a branch!

The next day they went even closer!

They plucked the fruit from a branch!

They looked at it!

They smelled it!

They ate it!

Oh no!

Now what?

God knew what they had done.

There was no place to hide!

God was *so* disappointed.

He still loved Adam and Eve.

He loved them very much.

But they had disobeyed!

So God told them

that they had to leave the Garden of Eden.

God told the serpent that from then on

he would have to crawl on his belly

—in the dust!

An angel showed Adam and Eve the way out of Eden.

The gate slammed shut behind them!

They turned around to look.

The angel was guarding the gate with a flaming sword!

They could not get back in!

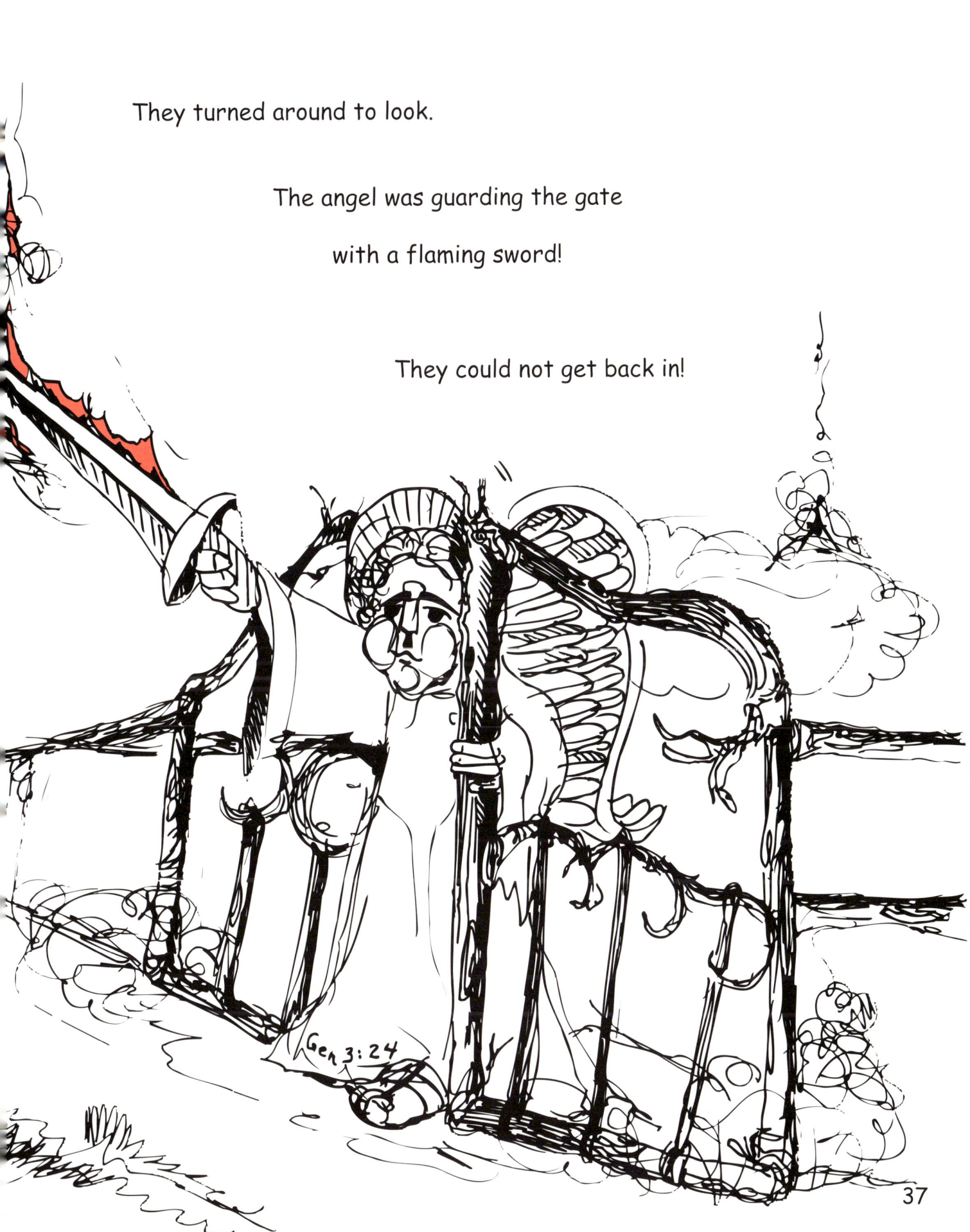

Inside the Garden of Eden,

everything was perfect.

It was paradise.

The earth grew no thistles to pinch their skin.

Roses had no thorns to prick their fingers.

Bees did not sting!

Dogs did not bite!

No one was ever sad!

Outside of Eden

everything was different.

There were many good things,

but there were also thorns and thistles.

There was danger...there was pain.

Everyone had to work very hard.

There was sometimes sadness.

Adam and Eve were afraid!

What would they do outside of Eden?

How could they live away from God?

Everyone born after Adam and Eve

would live outside of the Garden of Eden also—

like you and me.

How could we live away from God?

But God promised

that one day He would send a Savior.

The Savior would show everyone

the way back to God and Paradise.

When the time was right,

    God kept His promise.

      His *Bubbly, Gurgly, Overwhelming, Overflowing Love*

    began to bubble and gurgle and foam yet again!

      It simmered and spattered and popped.

        It gurgled and boiled and rocked.

          It splished and splashed and spewed.

            It overflowed as never before.

Because of His amazing love,

    God sent His Son Jesus

        to be the Savior He promised.

Jesus Christ came to earth

    as a little baby.

    His mother's name was Mary.

        She is called Theotokos, or Mother of God.

        She was blessed by God

            because of her great love, faith and obedience.

When Jesus grew up

He tried to teach everyone about God's Kingdom.

He told them to love one another,

...to smile and to share,

...to try to do what pleases God.

Some people loved Jesus

    because He brought joy to their lives.

Some people hated Jesus

    because they wanted to do things their way!

Hate causes people to do very bad things!

One sad, sad day,

    those who hated Jesus beat Him with a whip.

    They hurt Him very badly!

    They nailed Him to a Cross!

Mark 15:15-25

    Jesus could have called thousands of angels

    to help Him,

    but He didn't!

Jesus Christ died on the Cross.

All of God's Creation was very, very sad

because He did not deserve to die.

The sun stopped shining.

The earth began to tremble and to shake.

Mt 27:45,51

The earth shook and it shook and it shook.

It shook so much

that the gate to paradise burst open!

Because the Son of God willingly died on the Cross,

everyone now has a way back to God!

Joseph of Arimathea and Nicodemus

took Jesus off of the Cross.

They buried Him in a tomb.

Three days later,

Mary Magdalene and her friends

went to the tomb where Jesus was buried.

It was empty!

A bright, shiny angel was in the tomb.

The angel smiled at the women and said,

He is not here.

He is risen!

Go tell His disciples:

Jesus is Alive!

No one could believe the great news!

But sure enough, soon Mary Magdalene saw Jesus alive.

The Apostles saw Jesus alive.

All of Jesus' friends were very happy!

They felt *God's Bubbly, Gurgly,*

Overwhelming, Overflowing Love

oozing and squishing

and filling their hearts with great joy!

Soon Jesus told His friends

that He had to go back to His Father in Heaven.

But He said that they should never be afraid!

He promised to send the Holy Spirit.

The Holy Spirit would be with them always!

The Holy Spirit would give them power

to do everything God wanted them to do.

The Holy Spirit would fill their hearts

with as much of

God's Bubbly, Gurgly, Overwhelming, Overflowing Love

as they would let in.

Before He left,

Jesus told them to tell everyone the Good News!

The Good News is that

Christ is Risen!

The gate to paradise is open!

More Good News:

If we are Baptized,

    we are a part of Jesus Christ.

        We belong to Him!

If we try to be like Him,

    and receive Holy Communion often,

        we stay a part of Him.

            We become holy—like Him—

                just as the Saints did.

        If we are a part of Jesus Christ

            —who is alive—

                we never really die!

The Best News:

If we belong to Jesus Christ,

some day, when our life on earth is over,

we will go to be where He is.

We will live in Paradise

—a special place called Heaven—

with God, the heavenly spirits, the Saints,

and everyone who loves God.

In Heaven, God will wipe away every tear.

His love will bubble and gurgle and foam everywhere.

Bees will not sting!

Dogs will not bite!

There will be no thorns, no thistles, no danger!

No one will hate anyone.

No one will ever grow old.

There will be no more sin,

no more suffering,

no more sorrow,

no more pain,

no more death.

All around will be bubbling rivers and gurgling waterfalls,

beautiful flowers and towering trees.

Lions and tigers and lambs will be our friends.

We will play with reindeer and koala bears,

whales and elephants,

and even cobras.

God's Bubbly, Gurgly, Overwhelming, Overflowing Love

will continually bubble and gurgle and foam.

It will simmer and spatter and pop.

It will gurgle and boil and rock.

It will splish and splash and spew.

It will jiggle and jangle and jam.

It will overflow and fill our hearts--

FOREVER!

Rom 8:38-39

Try always to be like Jesus!

If you make a mistake,

pray: I'm sorry God!

Please help me to do things your way.

God loves you!

If you are really sorry

He will forgive you!

THEN JUST KEEP ON TRYING!

This is a prayer for any time:

when you are lonely or frightened,

when you are happy or sad,

when you've been good or when you've been bad.

Pray it over and over!

The Jesus Prayer

Lord, Jesus Christ,

Son of God,

have mercy on me!

When you were Baptized,

    God gave you your very own Guardian Angel

        to guide you and to guard you.

If you listen very carefully,

    you will hear a little voice in your head

        telling you to do things God's way.

    —that's your Guardian Angel!

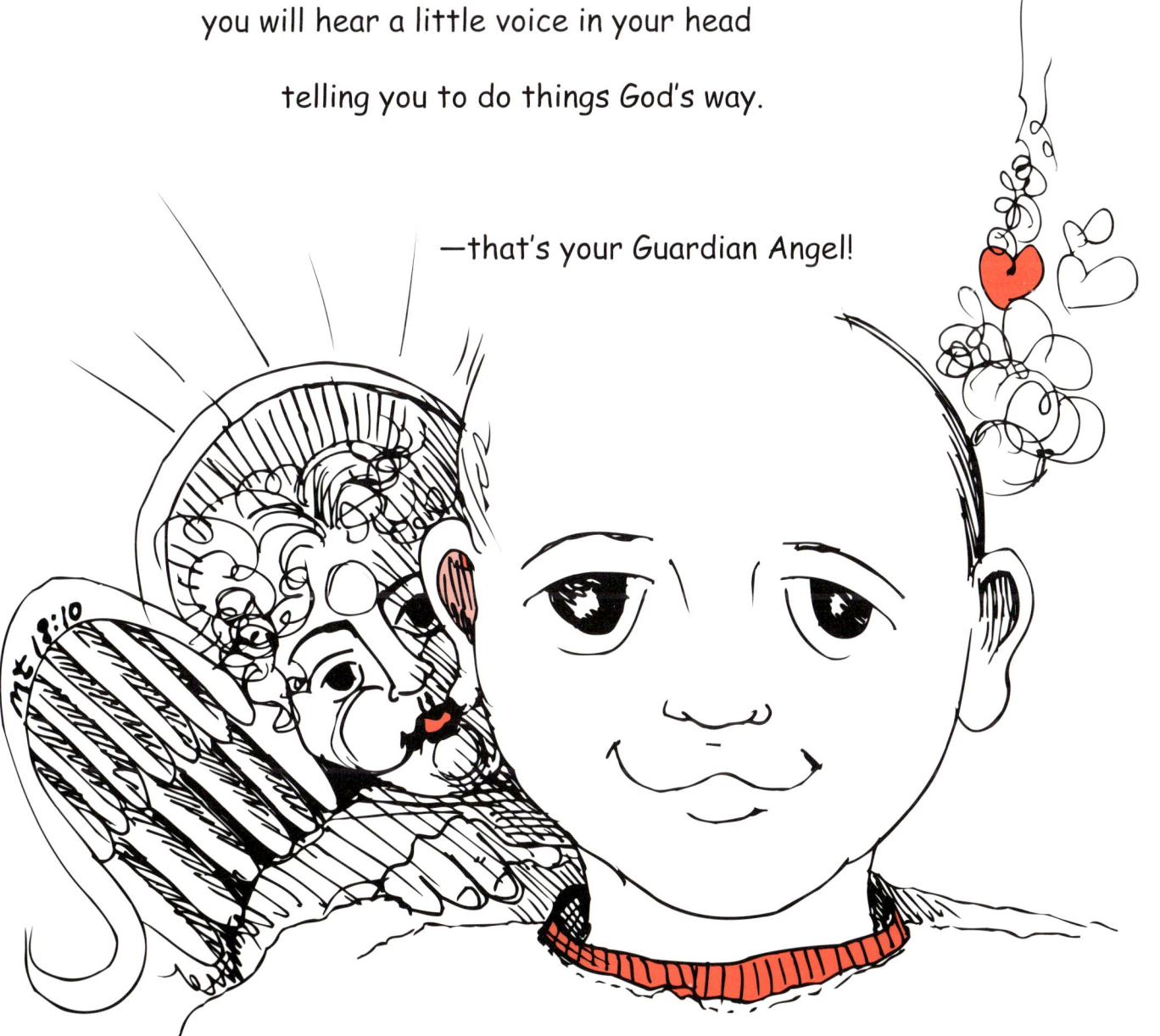

Always listen to that little voice

and pray this special prayer:

Oh Angel of God, my holy guardian,

given to me from Heaven,

please protect and enlighten me this day.

Give me strength to overcome temptation

and save me from all evil.

Teach me to do what is right

and guide me in the steps of Christ, my Savior.

Amen.

Questions from Kids

—with help for the adults

who will answer them.

Let the child set the pace. Answer questions as they arise,
to the extent he or she can comprehend. Each reading will produce
more thoughtful reflection and opportunity for spiritual growth.

Why is there a triangle throughout this book?
The triangle symbolizes the mystery of the Holy Trinity: God the Father, God the Son and God the Holy Spirit (Gen 1:26; 1 John 5:7). Any way you read the one on the fifth page of *The Beginning*, backward, forward or inside-out, it reminds us that God was not created—He has always existed.

Who are the Cherubim and the Seraphim?
They are heavenly spirits who surround God's throne and sing praises to Him.

God created nine classes of heavenly spirits or celestial beings. They are named according to their function and are divided into three choirs: Seraphim, Cherubim and Thrones, who devote themselves to the love and adoration of God; Dominions, Virtues and Powers, who govern space and the stars; and Principalities, Archangels and Angels, who do God's will on earth as His messengers and our guardians (Ezek 10:5; Col 1:16; Eph 1:21). All celestial beings are bodiless in Heaven. Angels take on bodies only when they come to earth to do God's bidding. St. Paul wrote: *Do not forget to entertain strangers, for by so doing some have unknowingly entertained Angels* (Heb 13:2).

Why didn't God just leave the "Tree of Knowledge of Good and Evil" out of the Garden of Eden?
Out of His great love, God created Adam and Eve in His image (Gen 1:27), which means that they had free will, as He does. All He asked in return was their love—the only thing that was truly theirs to give. Demonstration of love requires choice. The presence of the Tree of Knowledge of Good and Evil in Eden gave Adam and Eve the opportunity to demonstrate their love for God by using their free will to choose obedience.

God gave each of us free will also—so we have choices to make. There are things that God tells us to choose to stay away from, for very important reasons: (1) to give us a way to demonstrate our love for Him; (2) to protect us—whatever He tells us to do is for our own benefit—physically, mentally, and/or spiritually; (3) to set us apart as belonging to Him: holy (Greek: agios).

Why was the serpent in the Garden of Eden?
God allowed Satan to work through the serpent to entice Adam and Eve to disobey the one rule He had given them—thus testing their faith and love. Satan had been the Angel of Lights, Lucifer, who was permanently evicted from Heaven because of his jealousy and greed. He then selfishly tempted Adam and Eve to prevent them from enjoying that which he had lost.

We all face situations that entice us to disobey God. He allows us to be tempted but does not leave us on our own. If we ask Him to, He provides strength to overcome every temptation. We have many friends in Heaven. We can pray to Jesus Christ and the Holy Spirit for help and can ask the Theotokos (the Mother of God) and the Saints in Heaven (as well as those on earth) to pray for us.

What are saints?
A saint is anyone who believes that Jesus Christ is the Son of God and who continually tries to follow His example in all things, thus growing in holiness (1 Cor 1:2). The stories of the lives of the Saints, who have come from every walk of life and have gone on to be with God, can inspire us to dedicate our lives to Christ as they did.

If Mary is Jesus' mom, why is she called "Mother of God?"
Theotokos is a Greek word which means "God Bearer." She is called God Bearer, or Mother of God, because she gave birth to the second Person of the Holy Trinity: God the Son (Heb 1:1-6, 8-12).

What happened to Adam and Eve?
When they died, because they disobeyed, their souls went to Hades, far from the goodness of God, as did the souls of everyone who lived and died before Christ was crucified (except Enoch and Elijah: Gen 5:24, II Kings 2:1-11). After Jesus' Body was buried in the Tomb, His Soul descended into Hades

(Eph 4:9) to give everyone who lived and died before His ministry on earth the opportunity to acknowledge Him as the Savior, Who could provide the way back to God. The icon of Christ's Descent into Hades (also called the Resurrection) shows Him lifting Adam and Eve out of misery to live with Him forever.

From the time of Christ's Descent into Hades, the souls of those who demonstrate faith in and love for Him during their lives do not go to Hades when they die. Instead, they experience God's Kingdom while awaiting Christ's Second Coming to earth. Then, because they belong to Him (part of the Body of Christ, the Church) through Baptism and a life of faith, they will receive new bodies and will live with God forever in Heaven, which will be even more wonderous and joy-filled than the Garden of Eden.

Why is a lamb shown walking to the Cross on page 43?
To remind us that Jesus Christ was the Lamb of God (Isa 53:7; Jn 1:29; Rev 5:6-10; 7:9-10; 12:11).

God's people, the Hebrew nation (Israelites), had been slaves in Egypt for 400 years. At last, God told Moses to tell Pharaoh to let His people go. But Pharaoh refused. God then sent nine different plagues, which brought suffering to the Egyptians, to try to change Pharaoh's mind. After the onset of each plague, Pharaoh begged Moses to tell his God that if He lifted the plague the Hebrews would be freed. But each time God lifted the plague, Pharaoh changed his mind. Finally, God offered Pharaoh one last chance. He warned that if the Hebrews were not freed, the first-born of every Egyptian household would die. He told His people to kill a young, perfect, male lamb and to spread its blood around the doorways of their homes. On the appointed night, when the Angel of Death went through the town on his mission, he "passed over" those homes marked with the blood of the lamb. The first-born in those homes did not die because they had obeyed God's instructions. God told the Hebrew people to remember this special night every year in a celebration called "Passover" (Ex 7-12).

Just as the obedient Israelites were saved by the blood of the Passover lamb, those marked with the Blood of Christ, the Lamb of God (through Eucharist and a life which demonstrates faith), will only pass through death to live forever with God (Jn 6:53-56; 1 Cor 11:23-30).

Is the gate to Heaven still open?
Yes! It will remain open until Jesus Christ comes to earth again to judge the living and the dead.

At the time of Christ's Crucifixion, there were two very special areas in the Temple in Jerusalem, where God's people, the Israelites, worshiped Him: the Holy Place and the Most Holy Place. God was present among His people in the Most Holy Place (Ex 25:21-22, 26:34), but because of disobedience (sin), they had no direct access to Him. God had given Adam and Eve one rule to follow. To teach the Israelites what sin is, in a world where people had strayed further from Him, God gave them 613 laws (the Mosaic Law). Every failure to follow the Law necessitated that they offer sacrifices (sometimes of animals) at the Temple in the Holy Place so they would learn that sin required atonement. A veil separated the Holy Place from the Most Holy Place (Ex 26:33-34), symbolizing the fact that through sin man erected a barrier between himself and God—a barrier he was unable to tear down by himself because each sacrifice to atone for disobedience was followed by more disobedience, in a never-ending cycle.

Jesus Christ was sinless—He did not deserve to die. Yet Satan conspired to have Him put to death. Under God's final Blood Covenant with His people, He accepted Christ's blameless death as final atonement, once and for all, for the sins of mankind. Thus Christ, the Lamb of God, was also the last living sacrifice under the Mosaic Law. At Jesus' death, the veil in the Temple tore in two (Mt 27:51) because the barrier between God and man had been removed.

Personal salvation requires faith that Christ is the Savior who thus provided the way to the Kingdom. This faith must be demonstrated as well as confessed (1 Jn 3:18-24). The way to demonstrate faith is to try always to live a Christ-like life, which is also preparation for eternal life with God in the fullness of His Kingdom, where all is holy. When the time is right, Christ will come to earth again to judge the faith of the living and the dead (2 Cor 5:10). After judgment, the gate will close again—permanently. The time of opportunity and testing will have come to an end.

What are "thistles"?
The thistle is a prickly plant. When touched, it leaves tiny slivers in the skin, which are painful and difficult to dislodge. There was nothing prickly in Eden, where everything was good. When Adam and Eve were evicted from Eden, they found themselves in a world that contained a lot of different kinds of thistles: all the potential difficulties and evils of life in a world that, for God's purposes (to teach, test and strengthen His people), includes Satan.

Thorns are also a part of life in our world. St. Basil wrote that in Eden the rose had no thorns, but afterward they were added to that lovely flower to teach us that "sorrow is very near to pleasure and to remind us of our sin, which condemned the earth to produce thorns" (*The Six Days*).

Why did Jesus come back to life after His Crucifixion?
To show us that there is life after death!

Up to the time of Jesus' Crucifixion, everyone who had lived had sinned (like Adam and Eve), so everyone deserved death (Gen 2:17; Rom 6:23). Because Jesus Christ is God (the second person of the Holy Trinity: God the Son) and because He remained sinless while in the Flesh, He did not deserve death. Death could not hold Him. He Resurrected. His Resurrection is the most important and triumphant Christian message because it proves that we can live forever with God. This is why, during the forty days after Pascha, we greet everyone we meet with the joyous words: *Christ is Risen!* (Mk 16:6) to which the traditional response is: *Truly He is Risen!*

What does the word "Pascha" mean?
Pascha is the Greek word for Passover, which is better than the word Easter (a pagan term) as the title for our celebration of the Resurrection of Christ. It reminds us that Christ was the Lamb of God (1 Cor 5:7; John 1:29).

Why, in this book, is the color red used to show both good and evil?
Everything God created was good. Evil comes from misuse of God's creation—turning good to bad. We used the color red to depict this graphically. Red is used on hearts, flowers and the triangle symbolizing the Holy Trinity, to depict God's love, but it is also used to emphasize Satan's craftiness and Adam and Eve's shame and loss of innocence.

Quoted scripture is from the New King James version of the Holy Bible, © 1984, by Thomas Nelson, Inc.

Love and gratitude to those who helped with and supported this project:

    Metropolitan Nikitas of Hong Kong, Rev. William S. Chiganos, Director of the Religious Education Commission of the Greek Orthodox Diocese of Chicago, Perry Hamalis, Dennis Garbis, Pauline Hamalis, Amy Sallas and Nola Vandarakis, all of whom read the manuscript and offered insightful comments;

    Ann Lampros, who offered technical advice; Linda Hardy and Scott Sanders, who generously spent many hours on the mechanical process; and Irene Boutzarelos, whose illustrations capture both theological truth and the child-like wonder of God's world;

    My husband, George, and daughters, Dheanna Fikaris, Michele Glavanovits and Laina Pappas Krabbe, who, as always, were my "sounding-boards," facilitators and encouragers.

The input of each enhanced the finished product. I pray that God will continue to fill their hearts and their lives (and mine too) with His overwhelming, overflowing love.